Contents

Picture Credits

Image on page 7: *Map of Leeds from 1895*
© John Hearfield (www.johnhearfield.com)

Images on covers & pages 15, 17, 21, 22, 23 & 24:
© Aireborough Historical Society (www.aireboroughhistoricalsociety.co.uk)

Preface

"With the movement today facing many of the gravest challenges and threats that it has faced in decades, it is important to look back on the history of the labour movement and those struggles which laid the foundations that we stand on today.

The Leeds Gasworkers strike of 1890 is one such struggle; when we look back on the actions of the workers in that dispute we can see some striking (no pun intended) similarity with the issues that affect trade unions today: issues of a rapacious and hostile government and of aggressive employers; issues of legality and employment rights; issues of how best to organise and how to find new & relevant ways of organising; and issues of political representation.

Today, of course, the objective conditions and the industrial landscape of Britain are very different. However, these are the key issues which trade unions in Britain and across the world are facing, and this pamphlet is an important contribution to the debate of how we take the struggles of today forward."

Joel Heyes, *Secretary of Leeds TUC*

Introduction

The past few years have seen a resurgence of the trade union movement, with one of the largest ever trade union organised demonstrations and large public sector strikes, as well as growing unrest in the private sector. The theme of this pamphlet is the upsurges of the union movement in the past, particularly around the textile and gas industries in West Yorkshire.

Around a hundred and twenty years ago there was the growth of the 'New Unionism' as workers in unskilled industry which was thought impossible to organise, proved the opposite of that. New unions organising workers in a wide variety of industries from textiles to the docks and many others sprang up, some winning great success, others less successful. Whilst the heart of this movement was in London, where the initial breakthroughs were made, it had powerful ramifications elsewhere.

In Leeds, it was these new unions, predominantly the gas workers, who organised the first May Day demonstration in the city, taking up the issue of the eight hour day. The Leeds Trades Council at that time was dominated by craft unions who were politically aligned with the Liberal Party who bothered little with such matters. Happily things are different today and the Leeds TUC lends its support to many struggles across the city and keeps the tradition of May Day going strong in its annual march.

Twenty years after that upsurge, following a period which saw the gap between rich and poor increase, a massive strike wave developed for better pay and conditions known today as the 'Great Unrest'. This period saw the first national strikes of railway workers and miners, and a whole number of famed disputes, including where the armed forces were used to put down strikes. There were a number of struggles in West Yorkshire and we present some less known, but just as bitter, disputes in this pamphlet.

These struggles are rich with lessons for today as we enter a period of tremendous struggles of working people to protect their interests from the onslaught of a capitalist

ILP mural in Bradford

class seeking to make workers pay for the costs of the crisis of their system. Workers today can draw huge inspiration from their tenacity, creativity and willingness to struggle to the end.

The time period covered also deals with another question; that of independent political representation as developed in the wake of the Manningham Mills strike. The development of this was not at all straight forward; in areas such as Bradford then electoral success was rapid, elsewhere it was a much more complex affair. The period between the struggles discussed in this pamphlet saw the creation of both the Independent Labour Party (ILP) in Bradford in 1893, and the establishment of the Labour Representation Committee (forerunner of the Labour Party, which the ILP became a component part of) by the TUC in 1900.

Although Tom Maguire, who we shall meet when we discuss the Leeds gas workers strike, had been agitating for a 'Socialist Labour Party' since 1888, there were still trade unionists tied to the Liberals come the beginning Great Unrest over 20 years later, especially some leaders of the miners.

Yet as the 1913 lockout shows, elected representatives, including local councillors, that genuinely represent the interests of workers can play a vital role in furthering workers struggles. As further stormy battles loom, working people will test the ideas of those who aim to represent them and, like the Liberals of old, will deposit into the waste bin of history those that do not measure up to the task.

Join us in the Socialist Party

www.socialistparty.org.uk
www.leedssocialistparty.wordpress.com

'The Battle of Leeds': The Gasworkers Strike of 1890

by Iain Dalton

The period known as the New Unionism, must go down as one of the most inspiring episodes in the history of the working class in Britain. Trade unions had traditionally been the preserve of a skilled 'labour aristocracy', but in the space of a few years unions that were tens of thousands strong sprang up amongst dockers, labourers, gasmen, match girls and others.

After the emphatic winning of the 8 hour day, with no loss of pay, at Beckton Gas Works, Will Thorne's union, the Gasworkers and General Labour's Union (GGLU), recruited heavily across the country as semi-skilled and unskilled workers saw the necessity to organise to win improved working conditions for themselves

Leeds was no exception. A small group of Socialists had been putting forward socialist propaganda for five years but had only grown at a very slow rate. However, when the wave of new unionism arrived they eagerly sought to build it further in the city. During the summer, after some building workers attended an open air Socialist League meeting at Vicar's Croft, they helped them organiser their fellow workmates and won increases in pay after a short sharp strike.

A GGLU branch was established and put demands forward which were granted almost immediately in Autumn 1889. They won an 8 hour day for stokers, firemen and coal wheelers, increases in pay, time and a half for overtime, a week's paid holiday for all permanent men and double time for Christmas Day and Good Friday. These concessions were to be put in practice immediately and further discussions were to be held over a permanent set of rules regarding pay and conditions.

Yet these discussions never took place and the council broke its agreement by refusing to pay double pay on Good Friday. Then, in June, the council posted up new unilaterally imposed working conditions to come into effect on July 1st, precipitating the strike. As Thorne explains "They demanded that the gas workers should engage themselves for a period of four months and forego their right to strike within that period. They also wanted the stokers to do twenty-five per cent more work during their eight hour shift than they had being doing." When Thorne arrived in Leeds he also found out that the council had "...decided to change the custom of discharging in the slack season the last men to be taken on in the busy season. They had given all the men in the retort houses their notices."

This had been a conscious plan of the council, Alderman Gilston, a Liberal councillor stated that their time 'would be in the summer' when they could 'make a permanent arrangement with the men', referring to the fact that the summer season required less work as the gas-lit lamps, for example, would be lit for a shorter period due to the lighter evenings.

By the second week of June none of the men had signed the new terms and the yardsmen had gone on strike in protest, with others to follow as they worked their notice period. This led managers and their assistants to attempt to do their job, desperate to build up a supply of gas before the rest of the workforce struck too. Between 12,000 and 14,000 attended a mass meeting on the last Sunday of June to rally the gasworkers and their supporters for the battle ahead.

The council's gas committee tried to break the strike by the use of scab labour to keep the gasworks running and a regular supply of gas to the city, starting from the last week of June. By the end of that week it was apparent that these wouldn't be found locally, so envoys were sent to places such as Manchester and London to find men. However, many of these men were not told that they would be strike breaking, or had been told that they would be working as building labourers.

Back in Leeds crowds had already gathered over the past few days preventing the setting up of marquees to host the scabs outside the New Wortley works. Therefore, to avoid trouble, instead of the scabs disembarking at the nearby Hunslet train station, they were instead taken to the central station and escorted to spend the night in the Town Hall (see map).

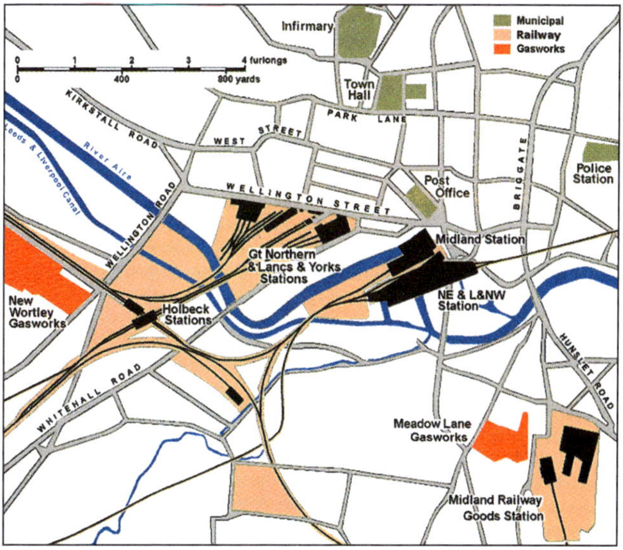

Map of Leeds from 1895

The 'Knockdown Blow'

The Meadow Lane works also had a nearby train station, and huge crowds gathered there to 'welcome' scabs in the drizzling rain. With the train being delayed and not arriving until the early morning then most of the crowd had drifted away by then, but returned quickly the next day to surround the gas works, with between 10,000 and 15,000 outside by 10pm. Earlier in the day protestors had climbed the walls of the works to call on the scabs to leave and most had done so, with the union offering to pay for their travel homes.

Meanwhile, the scabs who had stayed the night in the town hall were becoming restless, their haven had effectively become a police guarded prison. In an attempt to entertain them whilst plans were drawn up to get them to a gasworks, an organ recital was arranged, with Councillor Hunt from the gas committee signing 'Auld Lang Syne' and 'Rule Brittania'.

Expecting that crowds would attempt to stop them taking the 260 scabs to the New Wortley works, just over a mile away, the gas committee reinforced their escort with police from Bradford, Huddersfield and York, as well as foot soldiers and sixty mounted carabineers from Leeds barracks, making around 500 escorts in total. Although they had planned the march to set off at 4.30pm, before the city centre factories finished for the day, the carabineers were late so the march only managed to leave the town hall at 8pm pushing through a 30,000 strong crowd.

However, as they approached the railway bridge over Wellington Road the trouble began. Workers had made their way down the railway track from Holbeck station to the bridge and armed themselves with various items to use as missiles, as had men who climbed the roofs of buildings nearby. As the *Leeds Evening Express* correspondent put it "The scene that ensued SIMPLY DEFIES DESCRIPTION, bricks, stones, 'clinkers', iron belts, sticks, etc., were hurled into the air to fall with SICKENING THUDS AND CRASHES upon and amongst the blacklegs and their escorts".

They managed to get the scabs into the New Wortley gasworks, but in a state of demoralisation and besieged by the crowds. A similar situation prevailed at the Meadow Lane gasworks, with bottles and other missiles being thrown. The crowd even managed to pull the outer gate of its hinges! By Wednesday evening / Thursday morning only 150 out of 750 scabs who had been brought in by train remained in the two gasworks, with several having climbed the walls and joined with the protestors themselves.

This had a serious impact on the output of gas from the works. Many businesses in Leeds had machinery powered by gas, including clothing manufacturing, printing and even hotels and restaurants. On the night of the riot at Wellington road railway bridge, the Yorkshire Post had to be written by candlelight!

Rumours that the gas committee were to be threatened with legal action by companies for loss of business was an indication of how hopeless their position had become. As Thorne reports, "…after four days they (the Gas Committee) gave way, paid off the few remaining blacklegs, and reinstated all the strikers". This did come with a few minor concessions, a slight increase in production targets and the change from a weeks paid holiday to four days (Christmas Day, Good Friday, Whit-Monday and August Bank Holiday)

A great victory had been won, and one which stands in contrast to the rolling back of new unionism in many areas of the country as employers went on a counter-offensive.

Lessons of the Struggle

Undoubtedly, a key factor the effectiveness of the struggle was the mass picketing, which drew in many other workers from the town. The list of arrests gives an impression of the crowd, over half of them were under 25 years of age, from skilled trades such as tailors and upholsterers to unskilled ones such as bottlers and bill posters a real mix of the working class in the town.

This was a conscious strategy, Thorne reports that on hearing of the attention of bringing scabs to New Wortley, one of the strike leaders, Tom Paylor, chalked this on pavements in various parts of the town to encourage people to join the strikers in opposing the scabs. Decisive action was taken at each step, for example, Thorne had the last £300 the GGLU had in the bank put at the disposal of the strikers in Leeds. Such commitment to see the struggle through to the end motivated Fredrick Engels to present a copy of *Capital* to Thorne inscribed "To Will Thorne, victor of the Leeds battle…"

The key however, wasn't necessarily the widespread violence that took place, but the mass movement of workers that checked the attempts of the authorities at each step. It was that which led to huge numbers of police and soldiers been dragged into the dispute at huge cost, and the diversion of the scabs to the town hall due to the mass 'welcoming' presence outside the gasworks.

The appeals made to the scabs also played a role, facilitating them returning home and cheering when scabs left the works also fatally undermined the Gas Committee's strikebreaking attempts. Of course, Socialists support workers right to defend themselves. No doubt in the context of police lashing out at almost anyone in the vicinity of the gas works (as one business owner wondering why his gas-powered machinery wasn't working and found out to his misfortune – being sent to hospital after being hit by police a dozen times), then taking to the security of a bridge or rooftops and launching missiles must seem like a safer bet to try to arrest the progress of the scabs convoy than directly confronting the police and getting your head cracked open for your trouble.

However, after the strike, some sections of the movement demanded the immediate arming of workers and acts of violence against authority. Tom Maguire, one of the leaders of the Socialist League locally and one of those who played a key role in assisting the organisation of the new unions in Leeds, was scathing about this approach. In a letter to Edward Carpenter he wrote,

"Our Anarchist friends, who were conspicuous by their absence in the gas fights, joined issue with us at once, attacked not only the League but ourselves, and finally told the people that no policy should be entertained but physical force. Now, while I believe in the use of physical force when necessary I think that it is midsummer madness to advocate it on a public platform, and it is unlikely, as it would be undesirable, for the people to resort to it until other means had been tried and found wanting."

Political Representation

At the time of the strike the Liberals had an unrivalled political dominance in the town, with 30 councillors and all 16 of the aldermen, they also had 3 out of the city's five MPs. Despite many of these representatives being factory owners or other employers, they posed as the 'friends of the working man'. Their allies held dominance over the Leeds Trades Council, which at this time was mostly concerned with protecting the position of their craft members, rather than defending the interests of workers as a whole.

Yet these self-same 'friends of the working man' had not only attempted to drive down the living standards of the gas workers, but also were responsible for a series of public health failings around Leeds, some due to the unhealthy conditions around the masses of back-to-back houses that still dominate many inner city areas of Leeds to this day. At the strike's victory rally, George Kinton, of the Boot and Shoe Operatives, announced that a labour electoral league would be formed to challenge the Liberals at the upcoming council elections in November.

In the same letter to Carpenter quoted above Maguire makes the point that "I admit the Labour Electoral move is not at all to be desired, but it seemed the next immediate step to take in order to keep the Labour union militants, and to emphasise the conflict of the workers and the employers."

As a result, the socialists and new unionists around Maguire took a number of steps toward promoting independent labour candidates, inspiring the same move to take place in Bradford which ultimately led to the formation of the Independent Labour Party in 1893. Yet such immediate success as in Bradford, with a Labour councillor elected in 1892, was not replicated so quickly in Leeds where the first Labour councillor was not elected until 1903.

This indicates how closely the development of working class political representation is linked to struggle. Whereas an electoral challenge was mounted straightaway after the defeat of the Manningham Mills workers, in Leeds the attempt to develop independent political representation became straddled between the Lib-Lab-ers who dominated the Trades Council leadership and wanted to push labour candidates through the Liberal Party and the new unionists who wanted independent workers representatives.

The first real attempt at a challenge came at the 1981 council elections, a year and a half after the strike, where two failed Trades Council nominees to the Liberal party and Cockayne of the GGLU stood, with two of them achieving votes close to the Liberals. Yet this went no further having served the Lib-Lab-ers purpose of merely threatening the local Liberal leaders, and indeed they strangled further attempts such as putting forward a candidate in the South Leeds by-election in 1892.

The path to winning genuine working class political representation can, as in Leeds, sometimes be a tortuous one, with those clinging to inadequate existing political vehicles that have long since served their usefulness forming one obstacle. On the other hand, opportunities can slip by because of lack of preparation and other factors which if otherwise exploited could see big leaps forward. The key for socialists is to link their battles together, both on the industrial and political planes, and push for as wide a presence as possible in each field of campaigning for a better society.

References

- Hearfield, J. 'The Leeds Gas-workers Dispute'
  (available online - www.johnhearfield.com/Gas/Gas_strike.htm)
- Hendrick, H. 'The Leeds Gas Strike, 1980' *Thoresby Society Miscellany*, Vol.16, Part.2 pg.78-98
- Renton, D. 'Tom Maguire: Classical Marxist?
  (available online - www.dkrenton.co.uk/research/maguire.html)
- Thompson, E.P. (1967) 'Homage to Tom Maguire' in Briggs, A. & Saville, J. (eds) *Essays in Labour History*, Macmillan: London
- Thorne, W. (1989) *My Life's Battles*, Lawrence and Wishart: London

Manningham Mills 1890-1891: A strike that changed Britain's unions

by Manny Dominguez

Manningham Mills, owned by Samuel Lister, was one of the largest factories of its kind in the world. It employed 5,000 workers, the majority women. On 9 December 1890 Lister posted a notice outlining reductions in pay for weavers, pickers, spoolers and winders, hitting 1,100 workers in total. Lister threatened a lock-out if workers did not accept.

Company managing director Jose Reixach blamed deteriorating economic conditions in British and foreign markets for the textile industry's decline. For example, new tariffs had effectively closed US markets to Lister's fabrics. Tariffs or taxes on foreign imports were a form of protectionism, introduced by governments that hoped to lessen the impact of the global economic decline by trying to boost national economies.

Reixach also claimed that, up to then, workers had been paid 'unnaturally high' wages! Lister previously had a virtual monopoly on velvets and plushes. He argued that

Listers Mill in Manningham

when Britain dominated the world market in textiles, the employer could afford to pay better wages. However with a much weaker world economy, the employer said, workers must accept more 'realistic' wages. Sound familiar?

Strategy for action

The workers' reaction was predictably hostile. Few were in a union but were prompted to invite regional officials from the Weavers Textile Workers Association to discuss a strategy for action. From the first meeting a Work Peoples' Standing Committee was appointed to negotiate a settlement with the employer.

After negotiations drew a blank, the workers convened again. A third official from the union, Ben Turner, a socialist, compared Manningham workers' wages to other local textile workers - and to company profits. In the previous year, Lister's profits were £138,000. Turner argued that a wage reduction would save them only £7,000 a year or 5%. But if Lister carried out the wage cuts, workers would be 20% worse off.

During meetings with management on 16 December, workers argued that the employers' yearly averages of workers' pay hadn't taken into account earnings lost due to 'broken' or 'waiting time'. Management, however, refused to budge. Despite union officials urging caution, the workers called for strike action.

Workers were ill-prepared for industrial action; they had no strike fund and indeed no formal union branch structure. The striking workers' priority was not only to spread the issues and get support, but also to establish a strike fund.

A manifesto was written. Women, who were most of the strikers, went out with children across northern England and Scotland collecting donations for the strike fund. Processions became a regular Thursday fixture in Bradford. Messages of trade union solidarity came from across the world. Money paid for the strike fund supporting workers and their families and for food and food kitchens but harsh weather made life very hard.

By the end of March 1891, all 5,000 workers were out. The tempo of processions, meetings and demonstrations increased, especially when the dispute spilled onto the political arena. The actions of Bradford council, the police, the Watch Committee (who controlled the police) and Poor Law Guardians further politicised the dispute.

The 1834 Poor Law criminalised the poorest in society. Unemployed people applied for poor relief to the Guardians of the Poor Law. Strikers were denied poor relief if they refused to be blacklegs (scabs) and work at Lister's Mill. The Guardians (ie the council) saw them as undeserving for refusing to work.

The police bussed in scabs and sometimes used unnecessary force against the pickets. When management of the venue where the trade union movement held many meetings told them they could no longer use it, they were furious. The Watch Committee said they could not hold meetings in Bradford unless the unions stopped their regular Sunday meetings.

The Strike Committee opposed this unjust attack on free speech and assembly. On 12 April Bradford Trades Council organised a rally and requested the use of Dockers' Square for an overflow meeting. The Watch Committee refused.

The next day left groups called on people to assert their right to public assembly at that Square. Thousands gathered in the streets and the military were drafted in. The next mass protest meeting on 19 April was peaceful and attended by up to 90,000 people who passed a motion condemning the Watch Committee and demanding the right to assembly in the town centre.

Unfortunately the strike was on the verge of collapse. Financially, the strikers had difficulty in sustaining the dispute even though the number of strikers had increased. The employers would not compromise. Lister rejected the Strike Committee's final offer to submit to arbitration. All this undermined the determination to resist of strikers who were being starved into submission.

Hardship, the threat of bailiffs and evictions and the hostility of Bradford's establishment weakened the strikers' resolve and their unity. On 22 April the spinners, the last department to join the strike, decided to return to work. On 27 April, the rest acknowledged defeat and returned to work.

Over-production

After the strike a newspaper reported that there were up to 200 'blacklegs'. But that number could only carry out basic maintenance work in the mill, which in full production employed 5,000. Ironically the strike was at a time of general downturn in trade. Over-production may have compelled Lister & Co to at least a partial closure of the mills, so there was no urgency to resume to full production, which finally broke the strike.

The 1890s were a critical time in the development of the working class. Britain's economy had previously dominated world markets. Many workers had shared in this prosperity and working class organisations were dominated by more moderate, often purely craft-based, trade unions and co-operative societies.

After the radical Chartist movement in the 1840s, most leaders of the working class accepted capitalism. They worked to increase their share of the profits by increasing wages, lowering hours and improving working conditions and gave up ideas of changing the system.

These leaders saw the openly capitalist Liberals, worshippers of the free market and free trade, as the party to take workers forward. But by the late 1880s, growing industrial unrest made it clear that the period of liberalism as a mouthpiece for the working class was coming to an end.

Meanwhile, competition from emerging economies such as Germany and the US ensured that Britain would no longer be the 'great workshop' of the world. With rising costs for new machinery and falling prices for goods, industry tried to maintain its profits through cutting workers' share of the wealth by reducing wages, destroying jobs or both.

There was also a new political and industrial direction. The growth of the less craft-dominated 'new unions' was promoted by socialists, who injected a new militancy into the unions. They also questioned the whole social and economic system and criticised both establishment parties. With Friedrich Engels among them, they called for the creation of an independent working class political party.

Textile industry

The Manningham Mills strike reflected the economic and social relationships of the 1890s. The debate over wage rates and averages brought to the surface grievances affecting the whole textile trade such as loss of earnings due to 'broken time' and unhealthy working conditions.

Trade unionism was not strong in the textile areas in 1890. The multiplicity of processes in woollen textiles and in the velvet and plush trade created distinct groups of workers within each factory. Employers could often create divisions and prevent united action. Lister & Co tried this by proposing reductions which would at first only affect one quarter of their employees.

As women were the majority in the workforce, the Manningham Mills strike showed women workers were as militant as their male counterparts. It was an unprecedented display of militancy and unity in an industry where, previously, workers were neither militant nor united. Trade union membership in West Yorkshire rose rapidly.

The strike showed that the wider working class needed greater strength and unity both industrially and politically. A month after the dispute, Bradford Labour Union was formed, and the Independent Labour Party was formed in Bradford in 1893.

Even today, there are many similarities with the political and economic situation of this strike, not least the desperate need to create a new mass workers' party to represent the workers not the bosses.

Mill workers

Riots, Lockouts and Hunger Strikes: Class Struggle in Yeadon 1909-1913

by Iain Dalton

Aireborough to the north-west of Leeds is a semi-rural area covering the towns of Guiseley and Yeadon as well as the village of Rawdon, separated by the ring-road from the main hub of Leeds and by the river Aire from Bradford. The area's main industry was in textile mills, particularly in Yeadon and Guiseley, the workers within there playing the leading role in establishing the trade union movement in this area, a reminder of this being the Factory Workers Club in Guiseley.

The textile industry in the area developed out of the cottage industry, with the first power looms installed in the 1860s and the cottage industry dying out two decades later as more mills were established. Alongside the development of 'new unionism', the Yeadon & Guiseley Power Loom Weavers Union was established in 1887, like many other textile unions being craft-based, but only a few years later broadened into a general textile workers union, eventually becoming the Yeadon, Guiseley and District Factory Workers Union (YGDFWU) and affiliating to the Yorkshire Textile Workers' Federation. Additionally, the linked industry of textile dyers was organised by the Amalgamated Society of Dyers, which was a national trade union which had members active in the area.

Although YGDFWU membership had declined around the turn of the century due to a slump within the local textile trade it had recovered since then, reaching a membership of 393 males and 297 females, with the union pushing various wage claims for different sections of workers.

The Great Unrest, of 1911-14, was the backdrop to the lockout of the Aireborough textile workers. A Liberal government had been elected in 1906 on a radical programme of opposing the 'landlords, brewers, peers and monopolists'. The new government initially passed new progressive, although limited, welfare measures and enacted legislation giving unions immunity from being sued when taking industrial action (which had been allowed by the recent Taff Vale judgement).

But the period as a whole was one where, despite economic growth, real wages were declining and the gap between the rich and the poor increased. Discontent grew as the masses became disillusioned with the Liberals, despite their re-election in 1910, and a massive strike wave developed against poor working conditions, vicious management discipline and the decline in real wages. Around the same time as the 1913 lockout, local newspapers report that boot & shoemakers and joiners in Guiseley were on strike, as well as some council workers in Leeds, and a similar picture could be observed nationwide, including huge strikes of railway workers and miners.

The 'Old Dog' Strike

Prior to the events of the lockout, however, was the 'Old Dog' strike, four year previous. It began as a strike over pay and recognition of the Amalgamated Society of Dyers (ASD) at the Old Dog Mill run by the Yeadon Dyeing Company. The ASD in Yeadon had friendly relations with the YGDFWU and the two held occasional joint meeting as well as having an agreement for joint action (they would eventually be part of the same union, the National Union of Dyers, Bleachers and Textile Workers formed in 1936).

In the months running up to the strike the union had been gaining members in the mill, predominantly under 25s who held a meeting two days prior to the strike to discuss wage demands. After the provocative sacking of a union activist, 28 men walked out, to be joined by a further three, a majority of the shop floor staff. The company responded by declaring that all those who had walked out could consider themselves 'left' if they did not return by the end of the week, and refused any negotiations. Only three local men remained working at the mill, Long, Slater, and John Sturdy, a foreman, and brother of Thomas, one of the leading strikers.

Old Dog Mill after 1906 fire

Although the company advertised for scab labour, no-one from Yeadon would apply and the scabs had to be hired from further afield and picked up by wagonettes at Guiseley railway station each morning. Mass pickets were mounted at the gates of the factory to attempt to stop the wagonettes, not just by the strikers, but the wider workers movement in Yeadon. As Booth describes "Local millhands would go straight from work on the day turn to the area around the gates of the Old Mill and wait for the blacklegs to emerge. Women and children also congregated and not always out of curiosity; some of the women were as vehement against the scabs and police as were any of the men."

The Use of the State

The role of the state, as a state run in the interests of the employers, was shown clearly in the dispute when extra police were brought in response to the mass pickets to protect the blacklegs and break the strike. This solidified the opinion of the town against the employers, as Herbert Lockwood, secretary of the YGDFWU expressed when writing on behalf of that union in support of the ASD to the West Riding Joint Standing Committee.

"This committee desire respectfully to protest against the importation of such a large number of police, as they are of the opinion that it will tend rather to foster a feeling of resentment, instead of one of respect for the law.

"Their point is, that the dispute (Industrial) might be settled quicker and more satisfactorily if the forces of law were not so much in evidence; strengthening, 'as they do', the belief that they are sent to defend the Employers rather than to keep the peace."

Allied with this was an attempt by the employers to use the courts to attack the union. At first a case was brought by John Sturdy, using the company's solicitor, against two of the strikers for intimidation. The following week the company took two strikers to court, on the absurd grounds of that because the scabs the company had hired to replace them were not as skilled at cutting materials they were responsible for the company having some damaged goods!

The Yeadon Riots

It was a combination of this harassment by the law, as well as a feeling of frustration as union funds dwindled without any seeming breakthrough that led to what became known as the Yeadon Riots which took place from Saturday 11th to Tuesday 14th December 1909. On previous Saturdays the scabs from outside the area hadn't worked, but this time they were escorted in a wagonnette by the police they would on other working days. Unaware of this, the strikers hadn't organised a mass picket, although locals jeered at the scabs as they passed.

It was then that the first of two incidents between police and protestors took place. As Enoch Myers was returning from work in a nearby mill he was struck on the head by a projectile thrown by a scab. He immediately retaliated and was arrested by the police and taken into the Yeadon Dying Company office by the police before being released (no action was taken against the scab who threw the projectile).

After hearing about this crowds began to gather around the mill, whose patience was tested even further when the police blocked locals from using a public footpath that went past the mill. As the wagonnettes began their return journey to Guiseley train station, the crowds surged and a scuffle that saw a police Sergeant Bell have his shin kicked and one of the strikers, Herbert Marshall, was grabbed by the neck so hard it cut and started bleeding.

Some of the agitated crowd had also followed the scabs home, and began throwing sticks and stones at the window of two of their houses, smashing some windows before returning to the mill. Although there had been mass pickets and the scabs had been followed home before, that had been limited to verbal attempts to convince them to join the strike. It was only now on the back of intimidation and violence on the part of the scabs and the police that the crowds turned violent in frustration.

Attempts were made to storm the mill to get at the scabs still inside, this was repelled by the police, who then proceeded to escort the scabs home under a hail of projectiles of almost anything that was to hand. Pockets of people gathered outside not just the homes of the scabs in Yeadon, but also one of the mill owners, Fred Watson. The scabs houses were attacked (and Sturdy's was broken into) until they swore they would not return to work, as was Watson's and the crowd (which had now swelled to 2000) moved off towards Guiseley to do the same to scabs living there and the other partner in the mill, but were attacked by a large force of police and retreated whilst nursing injuries.

The following day further police were drafted into Yeadon and there were no further incidents until the Monday night when the imported scabs made their wagonette trip back to Guiseley where 500 gathered outside the factory, and more, smaller groups on the road to Guiseley determined to stop them. The wagonettes were pelted with stones by the crowd, one injuring the driver and further down a rope stretched across the road throwing one of the horses and the scabs had to flee the wagonnette and run for their lives.

The firm supplying the wagonettes then refused to supply them anymore, and the company's own covered van had to be used the following morning which again passed off without incident. However, in the evening a wagonette had been hired from Bradford to transport the scabs back home, which was intercepted by a picket who convinced the driver to turn back before arriving.

But as the crowd waited outside the mill a stone struck the Deputy Chief Constable commanding the police drafted into the area. He gave the order to the assembled police to charge the protestors, with mounted police clearing the Green opposite the mill and police attacking both those who had been protesting outside the mill and innocent bystanders. Staves were used to beat down anyone out on the streets. Even a man going into the Conservative Club was beaten. A guerrilla war of sorts took place in the twisting streets, alleys, yards and courts of Yeadon between the police and the population of the town as a whole.

Aftermath of the Strike

Despite bringing out the three Yeadon scabs and disrupting the transport on several occasions, the strike was by this point lost. The eventual agreement, which was accepted by the majority of those on strike, did see the union gain de facto recognition, although only 24 out of 33 strikers were given their jobs back and further negotiations between management and the ASD were to be held over wages and conditions.

Additionally, thirteen men were summonsed on charges arising from the riots, including all the members of the strike committee. This was clearly an attempt to hamper the ability of workers to organise in the area by attacking their leaders in the form of an amalgam, a term used by Trotsky to describe how real acts of sabotage in the Soviet Union and other events were tied to those who had nothing to do with them by false evidence and a biased court. Indeed, the evidence presented only referred to eight of those summonsed. Tried at the Leeds Assizes, one was found not guilty, all the others received between 2 and 6 months hard labour and became known as the 'Yeadon Martyrs'.

They and those who didn't get their jobs back at the end of the strike were de facto blacklisted. Union raised subscriptions for the family, despite union funds having been depleted and those who had been on strike running up debts with local trades people (which had been a factor in both the negotiations for the return to work and the frustrations expressed in the riots). The strike demonstrated the role of the state in siding with the employers (which due to the nature of the dispute in 1913, wasn't as much an issue as, with it being a lockout, the employers stopped running the mills during the dispute so there were not the same confrontations around scabs). But it also showed the tremendous solidarity that could be mobilised from the local community, which would be used to overcome the financial issues that had dragged down the Old Dog strike.

The 1913 Lockout

Despite the various issues action was being taken over during the Great Unrest, it was the claim for an improvement of the wages of Finishers, Dyers and Warehousemen on 3rd April 1913 that sparked the dispute. The union had been agitating over a few years for a standard wage rate across the industry, replacing the piece-rate system in some

Demonstration in Yeadon during the Lockout

areas of work that had developed out of cottage industry. The union opposed the piece-rate system as it exemplified the employers technique for all wages; employing the use of 'scouts' to go around the rest of the West Riding (of Yorkshire) and find out the lowest wages being made in other areas and then attempt to impose that on the workforce. The wage claim had been framed in a manner that would establish a flat rate for all 3 departments of work of 28 shillings a week for over 18 year olds. The employers instead offered a pitiful 1 shilling a week increase to finishers and warehousemen earning under 25 shillings a week, the dyers would get nothing.

Rejecting the offer, the workers in those departments took strike action beginning on Monday 19th May, solid except from the Nunroyd Mills in Guiseley which they swiftly started to picket. After two days of the police escorting the scabs in to work to protect them from the ire of the pickets, the employers posted up notice of a lockout commencing Friday morning if the dispute wasn't settled on their terms. By the end of the week 2,000 were locked out and a mass meeting of 1,000 was held in Yeadon Town Hall Square.

The following week, 1,500 workers marched from the town out to Yeadon Moor (now occupied by Leeds Bradford Airport) and within a few weeks the Willyers, Fettlers and Cloth Millers were also out, closing Crompton's Mill, one of the few still working in the area. With the employers convinced if they stood firm they could starve out the workers and break the union a compromise didn't seem likely soon.

Hunger Marches

In mid-June the first hunger marches started, marching out from Aireborough to nearby towns and cities appealing for support, which soon became a regular feature of

Locked out workers on hunger march

the dispute over the next few weeks, with at least ten taking place by the end of the dispute. The longest of these marches was of 30 men heading as far away as Blackpool (which raised £50 s8, around £3,000 in today's money, a total length of 174 miles) and a march to Leeds became a weekly occurrence with upto 300 walking the 7 miles to Leeds every Tuesday, whilst others went to Bradford, Huddersfield and Liverpool. All of the marches carried banners explaining they were collecting for the lockout fund and often had a brass band or other accompaniment.

A diary survives of one of the Blackpool Marchers, written by a John Preston. Despite receiving strong support during the march, some legs were hard, with the marchers getting drenched en route to Nelson, or having only a teacake to eat on the 31 mile leg on the return between Blackpool and Blackburn. In contrast, Preston writes that on July 24th they "Walked to Accrington, where there were 5000 on strike, and then to Baccup and Todmorden where the Socialists put their clubroom at our disposal. They brought up 25 loaves, 6 lbs cheese, 2 ½ lbs butter, and ¾ lbs tea and five jars of jam for our tea and breakfast. We had a meeting and a collection, and sent £7 home to Yeadon."

The marches were undertaken for a combination of reasons. The marches reached many other textile towns and labour movement groups bringing news of the dispute and allowing discussion to take place with workers in other districts (which would have different wage scales), sometimes marching specifically through other towns where disputes were taking place to show support for them.

The collections on the marches also helped towards alleviating the hardship of the locked out workers, with Lockwood reported in the press as announcing that donations tripled after the commencement of the marches. The money helped pay into a lockout

Hunger marchers on Town Hall steps

fund that was providing the workers with half-pay for the duration of the dispute, with soup kitchens and other support organised by local sympathisers, all of which played a role in making the dispute more protracted than the employers had bargained for. This also avoided the demoralisation which set in during the earlier Old Dog Strike from a lack of funds to sustain the strike. The acquisition a few years earlier of a union club (bought from the Liberals, a symbol of that parties decline in the area) also assisted in this, giving the union somewhere to organise from with impunity. Because the dispute was a total lockout, therefore making it unnecessary to mount picket lines, it allowed for the numbers to carry these marches out on such a mass scale in such a short time.

Political Representation

As the hunger marches showed, the workers were not short of support. The union had supported other disputes, even as far away as Russia, but one of the most crucial strikes in the local area had been the Manningham Mills strike twenty two year earlier, organising public meetings in solidarity with the strikers, inviting the strike leader over to speak and raising £49, 6s, 2d to support the strikers which was reciprocated in the dispute, with various forms of support including a loan of £75 from Bradford Trades Council to support the union hardship fund. But this was not the only thing the YGDFWU gained from their previous support of the Manningham Mills workers.

The most important lesson from that dispute was the need for workers to organise themselves independently from the Liberals and other so-called 'friends of labour' who would plead sympathy with the plight of working people but whenever those workers

Yeadon Liberal Club on election day December 1910. Symbolising the Liberals decline the YGDFWU bought this as their club in 1912 from which a soup kitchen was organised for locked out workers and their families

interests collided with those of the capitalist system they always supported the latter. This motivated workers in Bradford to establish the Independent Labour Party (ILP) in the years after the strike. Yeadon ILP had been established prior to the conference in Bradford which created the ILP as a national organisation, a major influence in this direction (and in the union) was Herbert Lockwood, who after being victimised by his employer in 1892 became the full-time secretary of the YGDFWU and was Yeadon ILP's delegate to the Bradford conference.

Yeadon ILP was not dissimilar from other local ILP groups in the area, it organised a variety of social events, but crucially it also organised education and agitation, producing its own journal, the Labour Chronicle from 1894 onwards and organised lunch-time and evening lectures, either with speakers from the local ILP or nationally like Keir Hardie, Ben Tillett, Tom Mann etc. to help educate their membership about the nature of capitalist society and other struggles taking place.

The ILP also spearheaded an electoral challenge to the masters with Lockwood being its candidate to the Wharfedale Board of Guardians in 1894 and also contesting elections for the local urban district councils, as well as assisting in establishing a Labour Representation Committee to challenge for the parliamentary seat of Otley.

By the time of the dispute, Lockwood was a member of the Yeadon Urban District Council and put this position to good use, establishing a distressed fund with money from a similar fund created during the 1912 coal strike, much to the consternation of the factory owners. Their response, however, was to pressure the council into passing a resolution calling on the trade unions to settle on the old wage scale (ie. a complete compromise) and arranging a conference of employers and the union on this basis.

Lockwood, who had walked out of the council meeting prior to the resolution being voted on was furious and criticised the council passing a resolution solely on the evidence of the employers without even consulting the workers.

The union used this incident to educate the strikes as to the role of those like the council and the local churches who were seeking to mediate between the workers and the employers, who as part of the state, bound by class ties and other factors whose first instinct will be to take the position of the employers. A later council missive calling for a ballot of weavers attracted a resolution from a mass meeting of weavers demanding that the council stopped interfering in the dispute in such a manner.

A Victory to Build Upon

Instead the next initiative from the council was far more neutral, calling a conference to discuss a settlement on the basis of the 'Dewsbury agreement' (a standard agreement in the Dewsbury district) with the proviso that 'non-essential' matters could be deleted. This resulted in a deal which saw a reduction in the working week, increased rates for overtime and night work, pay rises for sections of the workforce and clauses to cover training, meal breaks and other issues. However, the union did concede on the pay rise for the workers originally on strike (offset to a degree by the reduction in the working week) and on leaving the wages of 'infirm or otherwise incompetent' workers to be individually adjusted.

The deal was taken back to mass meetings of each section of the workforce where it was agreed to and signed. Despite the weaknesses of the deal, a general agreement covering all areas of the industry in the area was a big step forward for workers in Aireborough, particularly given the belief of the employers nine-weeks earlier that they could starve out and break the union. By holding mass meetings and discussing and elaborating the strategy and tactics of the dispute at each stage (union officials also travelled out to discuss with men on the longer hunger marches) they were able to weld together not just the union members, but also the much larger layer of non-union members who were involved in the lockout too.

As pointed out by the union leaders it was also a springboard which they should build on by recruiting and building the union, which they did. By the end of the year union membership had increased by 247, a 42% increase on the year before, eventually growing to 3,000 members by 1920 prior to amalgamation with the General Union of Textile Workers (negotiations had begun the year after the dispute but had been delayed due to World War I).

The experience of the lockout also highlighted the importance of independent political representation. At the rally to welcome back the last returning hunger marches, one speaker made the point that no assistance (financial or physical) had been received from either the Conservative or Liberal parties. Drawing upon this, Lockwood stated after the dispute, "[it would be] foolish for workers to organise trade unions and then vote against them at elections".

The ILP decided instead of just standing one candidate for the yearly council elections (councillors were elected for 3 years), they would stand a full slate for election. In the elections after the strike, Lockwood was up for re-election and topped the poll, with other Labour candidates coming 4th and 5th with strong results, although further progress was cut across by the war. Although the growing development of labour candidates would see the Labour Party returned to parliament as a serious force after World War I.

As we enter a period of similar stormy battles, workers will look with more scruple at the credentials and ideas of those who claim to represent them. Where they are found wanting, in the same manner as the Liberals, then workers and their representatives will increasingly look to stand candidates who fully back their own interests. In some unions such as Unite then this has meant backing suspended Labour councillors who carry out the union's policy of voting against cuts. The situation is however, more advanced in some unions who are consulting about standing their own candidates as the PCS union successfully consulted its membership on and the RMT union has been exploring through the Trade Unionist and Socialist Coalition.

References

- Macartney, P. (1991) 'The Yeadon Lockout and Hunger Marches of 1913' (available online at www.angelfire.com/ma/Socialworld/Yeadon.html)
- Booth, P. (undated) *The Old Dog Strike*, Otley & District Trades Council – available from Yeadon library
- Copies of the *Wharfdale & Airedale Observer* and the *Leeds Weekly Citizen* are archived at Leeds Central library can be viewed on microfiche
- There are also various resources available at Yeadon library that can be consulted including extracts from a marcher's diary.

The Tories Strike Back: Lessons of the Leeds Corporation Workers Strike 1913-14

by Iain Dalton

Throughout the period 1910-14, known as the Great Unrest, workers sought to push their wage claims forward to make up for stagnation in the previous decade. Just like in surrounding factory districts in nearby Aireborough, corporation (council) workers had not received a pay rise for some time in the summer of 1913. Whilst the Yeadon lockout was ongoing and holding weekly marches into the city, in Leeds itself 1,200 council workers took strike action with 867 of those workers receiving pay rises of between one and two shillings a week. Other workers took strike action in this period in the city, such as the boot & shoe operatives.

The victory of the initial strike of some council workers, and that of other workers elsewhere, in being able to push for across the board pay rises for workers in some sectors spurred a move to co-ordinate action between all the trade unions in Leeds council. Under the initiative of the Tramway and Vehicle Workers' Union, 8 trade unions came together in a Federal Council of Municipal Employees (FCME) with Arthur Gill of the Street Mason's and Paviors' holding the Presidency (as he did of the Leeds Trades Council).

The workforce of the council was somewhat different than from today, with two of the biggest groups of workers being public transport workers (on the no longer existent trams) and gas workers (also now in private ownership). However, similarities remain, at the heart of the June strike were 750 scavengers, who today we would call refuse workers and street cleaners, the same group of workers who took nine weeks of strike action in 2009 against pay cuts.

Yet all this had developed in a relatively recent period, under 25 years ago gas workers had been unorganised. The trades council was then in the hands of craft unions who generally felt above the struggles of semi and unskilled workers. Much had changed in Leeds in the intervening period, not least the establishment of the Leeds Labour Representation Committee, which changed its name in 1914 to the Leeds Labour Party with the backing of the overwhelming majority of unions and most local co-operative and socialist organisations.[1]

Yet in tactics reminiscent of a number of struggles, not least the 1984-5 miners strike, the employers, in this case the Tory-led council, delayed the dispute to a time more convenient for them, after the council elections due in November.

The workers, however, refused to accept this and at a mass meeting on September 21st demanded that their representatives be granted a meeting with the council, threatening to go out on strike from October 15th if this did not take place. Within days the FCME had backed them, and the GGLU balloted its 3000 members obtaining 2023 in favour and only 138 against. Yet whilst this did result in a meeting, it agreed to postpone the strike, leaving the workers almost at square one again.

In the run up to the election, Labour councillors argued for an inquiry into hours and wages, and forced the agreement that any approved claims be backdated to 1st October. The election saw a tipping of the balance in favour of the representatives of Labour, gaining 3 seats, plus a further one after aldermanic elections. However, due to the disproportionate number of aldermanic seats allocated to the Liberals, then Labour was still the third party in Leeds.

On 3rd December, an offer was approved by the city council which would give 1202 workers increases over two shillings and smaller increases of over a shilling for many others, only 239 involved in the dispute would receive no increase.

The Turning Point: Workers Reject the Offer

The turning point in the dispute came a few days later on 7th December when a mass meeting of council workers decided to reject the offer. Looking back from a period where workers are facing pay freezes, then some may wonder why workers would not be happy with substantial increases for most of the workforce. But this dispute was part of a stormy period where workers felt their strength after years of putting up with whatever breadcrumbs were offered.

Moreover, the bulk of the strikers were members of the GGLU which had beaten the council 23 years ago in the famed gas workers dispute and, unlike then, had the backing of the rest of the union movement through the FCME and Leeds Trades Council.

The strike began in high spirits on 11th December with some 3000 workers on strike, and another 1000 in the employ of the council were thrown idle. With the exception of the trams, all sections of the council workforce were affected, and the trams ceased operation when the workmen in the electricity stations joined the strike the following day.

At the same time the tramwaymen, who had their own separate agreement with the council which lasted until 4th August 1914, deliberated in the Co-op's People's Hall on Albion Street (now the entrance to Trinity Walk shopping centre). A crowded midnight meeting announced the result of the strike ballot where, out of 1229 members, 955 voted in favour of strike action with only 51 against. Their stoppage at midnight the following day brought the numbers out to 4292.

The most serious consequences of the strike was the lack of gas. Most Leeds factory workers went on short time as the factories were lit by gas, and work ceased altogether in sections of the clothing industry where gas was used for pressing irons as well as in a number of factories that used gas powered machines. Streets lay in darkness at night, and waste wasn't collected. Only a skeletal tram service ran. Life in the city was grinding to a halt.

The Tories Strike Back

Learning the lessons of other disputes in this period and previously, the Tories and their allies tried every means possible to break the dispute. William Walker Macpherson, the son of an engineer who inherited his shares in the business after his death, wrote to the conservative Yorkshire Post calling for a Citizen's League of Law and Order, modelled on an existing force of 1600 in Liverpool

To give an insight into the character of Macpherson, his family were part of an engineering firm 'Fairburn, Laweson, Coombe, Barbour and Company Ltd'. Their shareholding more than provided a comfortable living with expensive homes whilst Macpherson attended Leeds Grammar School and Yorkshire College (which became Leeds Uni) as well as studying in Paris and Germany. He was a manager at the Wellington Works until 1911 and in 1914 joined the Royal Field Artillery, staying on after the end of the war in 1921 in the period the British army was intervening in Russia and crushing the Irish rebellion.

As well as taking practical measures to establish such a strike-breaking force, the Yorkshire Post also established a fund for non-strikers which totalled £450 (Over £43,000 in today's money!) Clerks at the council were bullied into covering the jobs of strikers, threatened with dismissal if they didn't do so and bribed with an extra 7s 6d a day and compensation for spoiled clothing.

Some of the rare letters in the mainstream press from supporters of the strike demonstrate the lengths the council leaders were prepared to go to break the strike. One by an Ebenezer Wilcock in the Yorkshire Observer commented "Already the strike must have cost in positive expenditure and loss of revenue more than the £15,000 necessary to have paid the increased wages for a year..." Another letter in the Evening Post, entitled Meals for Workers, stated,

"Sir – I see in your last night's issue that the workers were provided with coffee and sandwiches. I was there and saw them get it after they had been working only 1 ½ hours. It is surprising what our council will do in a time like this. In ordinary times, if the workmen were working a double shift snowshifting they would not give them coffee, but if a man stopped to get a small tea the foreman would be on him asking how long he was going to stop

"One who wants Justice"

The local daily press consisted of five papers, all hostile to the strike; the Liberal papers *Yorkshire Evening News* (YEN) and *Yorkshire Observer*,[2] the Tory controlled *Yorkshire Post* (YP) and *Yorkshire Evening Post* (YEP) and the *Leeds Mercury* which wavered between Liberal and Tory views.[3] All of these papers printed articles attacking the strikers. Amongst their biased reports was one alleging that all the men at one gas works would report back to work the following Monday. Unfortunately for them, on this occasion, the Mercury was forced to report that in fact only a dozen had returned under the headline 'Expected Run Back of Men Does Not Take Place'.

The *Observer* went so far in a reply to a letter to justify their right to attack the strikers – "It cannot be said to be unfair that a newspaper has taken sides against the men and then has done all it can by argument and presentation of its views to defeat the strikers. That is legitimate journalism."

The YP and YEP were sometimes particularly vicious in their attacks, having features attacking GGLU leaders like Will Thorne, accusing him of being a syndicalist (he was unfortunately much more moderate) and lined with anonymous quotes from other union leaders denouncing him. They also slandered the Labour councillors, in the YP on 27th December alleging they were 'the most assiduous in finding berths for their workmen supporters', the same 'jobs for the boys' slander directed against the Militant-led Liverpool City Council in the 1980s during their battle against the Thatcher government.[4] In the main, however, they generally downplayed the effect of the strike more than the other newspapers. For example, reporting 400 at one strike meeting which the *Observer* gave the figure of 1000.

A mass of police was brought into Leeds to assist with breaking the strike. A photo which survives from the dispute depicts 20 officers from six police forces posing for a photo, with police constables as well as being drafted from nearby city police forces, coming from as far away as Liverpool. Every day the papers reported arrests and sentencing of strikers, some for harassing or threatening the scabs who were taking their livelihood, but many for trivial offences including obstructing the footpath and swearing!

One of the more controversial moves was the mobilisation of students and academics at Leeds University (only established 9 years earlier in 1904). Overall, two hundred students were used to scab on the strike, the majority (140) at the Meadow Lane gas works. Although this perhaps does not sound like many, there were only 663 full time students at the University.

When confronted Dr. Michael Sadler,[5] the Vice-Chancellor, argued that the university hadn't acted officially, however he stated his own opinion that individuals at the university had a duty to ensure the maintenance of public services, alongside other citizens – he also described the actions of the strikers as 'brigandage'. Despite Sadler's claim, indirect assistance to scabbing students was given by making special provisions for students absent from their exams. This is hardly suprising, given that A.G. Lupton, the Pro-Chancellor of Leeds University at the time, was the brother of Tory Alderman F.M. Lupton, a member of the special committee (see below).

This didn't go without challenge, with protests from trade union bodies and by a group of university academics, condemning the intervention of the university into the dispute. Sadler was particularly singled out, as he had previously promoted education for workers with the unions. The Trades Council cancelled Workers Education Association lectures with him speaking that were due to take place at the University and then his own Leeds branch of the WEA, of which he was President, condemned his actions during the strike and demanded his resignation.

Workers Unity Crumbled

However, it was the appointment by the city council on Wednesday 17th December of a Tory-Liberal special committee to pursue the dispute to the end which sealed the fate of the dispute. The committee was created with one goal; that of breaking the influence of the unions at the council, composed of 3 Conservatives and 2 Liberals, all were alderman rather than democratically elected councillors.

The special committee's first action was to issue an ultimatum to workers to submit applications for re-instatement by 6.30pm on the Friday, just two days away. On the Thursday a mass meeting of tramwaymen voted to return to work if allowed to do so en bloc and without having to cover for the work of strikers in the power stations. The GGLU, on the otherhand, ignored the ultimatum and restated its call for a 'conference with the Special Committee'.

The collapse of the united front across the council workforce put together through the Federal Council over the past few months was devastating. The workforce was split in half – 2028 workers, mostly tramwaymen, were reinstated. The rest remained on strike, whilst very protracted negotiations began. These started with an hour face to face at the Great Northern Hotel on Saturday 20th December, with the rest continuing by exchange of typewritten statements whilst the two sides remained in separate room – not a procedure conducive to resolving the dispute quickly. The result was that these negotiations broke off with an ultimatum from the special committee that it would only take back men by individual application.

In the few days before Christmas, the drift back to work continued, with 300 men making formal applications to return to work and other places being filled by newly hired scabs, there were just 1000 vacancies left. A special GGLU National Executive Council meeting took place on 29th December in Leeds to discuss the situation which increased weekly strike pay from 12s 6d to 15s and appealed for funds to other trade unionists nationally. At the same time repeated attempts were made to come to terms with the special committee, on 1st January the Federal Council offered to settle for only a one shilling a week increase for those who hadn't already received it, but the special committee were obstinate.

Despite some chaotic attempts to picket out other men and extend the strike, the momentum was lost as was the strike for all intents and purposes. JR Clynes MP, then union President, went into individual discussions taking place over four days (7th, 8th, 9th and 12th January) with the special committee. Over those days Clynes ended up giving up every aspect of the men's claim, the only concession he received in turn was that by settling the men would get preferential treatment for being taken back on by the council.

Only a few days before GGLU local official Walt Wood had stated that 'the corporation is beaten, absolutely beaten', therefore it was unsurprising that the men's response to the deal was to shout 'Twister!' and 'White Flag!' at Clynes when he reported the settlement to a mass meeting at 9am on 13th January. Clynes cowardly left out the fact that not all the men would be immediately reinstated as he had originally pledged to win, later admitting that he had explained the settlement in 'some of the more generous language' which the special committee members had used. Unsurprisingly, after the meeting reluctantly accepted the deal, therefore ending the dispute, Clynes caught the 11am train back to London.

The Lessons of the Dispute

Despite Will Thorne attempting to put a positive gloss on the dispute shortly after the strike ended, saying "We haven't won a victory and we don't think the Corporation have," it is difficult to agree with his conclusion. Whilst it's true the special committee didn't manage to break the union, this was due to the strike causing complications for some employers who depended upon gas, such as the Boot and Shoe Manufacturers who passed a resolution protesting against the special committee's intractability.

But workers ended up with less than they would have achieved if they had not gone on strike. Those who didn't return to work immediately didn't get the pay rise passed by the council on 3rd December back-dated to 1st October.

Although he also tried to put the same gloss on the dispute as Thorne, Leeds Trades Council secretary Owen Connellan's comments at the end of the dispute do give us more insight into the complications of the strike. He was quoted by the Leeds Mercury as saying,

"'In the circumstances,' said Mr. Connellan, 'I think the best plan was to accept the terms. The men might have put up a fight for a much longer period, and no doubt they would have been supported in their course, but the secession from their ranks made any continuance of the strike of rather doubtful advantage.

"The whole of the men were in a Federal Council, but some of them had absolutely nothing to gain; and it seems to me that there will always be a weakness in the ranks of strikers if sections of them do not stand to benefit from the strike."

This touches on some of the weakness of the dispute. Not only was the agreement of the tramwaymen with the council not up for review until August 1914,[6] but large sections of the workforce had already gained the level of increase that the union was fighting for. Therefore large sections of the council workforce were taking part in the strike in solidarity with other workers. As events showed, many crumbled under the pressure of losing their jobs and returned to work.

It is not that union leaders did not recognise the seriousness of the situation, with the Federal Council pointing out in a letter to the special committee that their proposed terms were effectively denying the right to collective organisation. A speaker at one of the union's mass meetings, Frank Fountain, was reported in the Observer as stating "…the fight was against a combination of all the employers in Leeds," and drew out the need for widening the strike.

Nor is it the case that they did not take measures to attempt to respond to this situation. The union did take steps to counter this drift, with the increases to strike pay implemented on December 29th, a step which had been mooted at a rally 5 days earlier. They also did try and broaden the strike, and indeed encourage the tramwaymen to rejoin the strike, however, such attempts are bound to be undermined when large sections of the workforce were returning to work.

However, a key part of leading any struggle is to be able to survey what could be possible to achieve given the objective situation, what is necessary to achieve that and then to make a judgement on whether to press forwards, or retreat in good order.

There were in reality two key turning points in the dispute, the decision to reject the partial concessions offered by the council on December 3rd and the ultimatum by the special committee on December 17th. By rejecting the offer of December 3rd then the council unions were preparing for an all out battle over this issue, a battle that became all too real with the ultimatum. Things that only happened later, such as appealing for funds from other unions across the country, should have occurred then given the seriousness of the dispute.

Likewise with the 17th December - this was really crunch time in the dispute. To secure victory it would have been necessary to expand the strike – which in itself would have given confidence to wavering members of the council workforce that they would not lose their jobs despite the special committee's threats.

Instead the strike leadership wavered, and the measures they took only slowed the collapse of the strike rather than acting as a launch pad for victory. Indeed, reading some of speeches of leading figures from the GGLU, especially Thorne and Clynes, it looks like they are trying to sound radical whilst desperately looking for some way to end the strike without losing face with the men.

Clynes in particular was seen as a vehicle by which the special committee thought they could get the men to accept their terms. Indeed the Special Committee accepted the negotiations with him '...in view of the known moderation of Mr. Clynes...' Thorne's role in the 1890 gasworkers strike was still remembered too well, despite his recent denunciation of Jim Larkin, leader of the Dublin Lockout, whereas the Yorkshire Post was happy to report that 'Mr Clynes was dead against the strike which has since taken place.' By distorting the terms of the settlement when he reported them back he broke a cardinal rule for those who claim to lead the workers movement, of 'saying what is', not lying or trying to sugar-coat a difficult situation.

In an all out dispute it is necessary to have a leadership that will prosecute the struggle to the end, and unfortunately this was not present in this dispute in Leeds. Workers should study the lessons of this and other disputes as well as testing out those who claim to lead them. Those who are found wanting in struggles, hesitating when action is required or distorting the situation, must be replaced by challenged genuine class fighters.

References

- The Macphersons of Leeds (www.reynoldmacpherson.ac.nz/publications/Macphersons%20of%20Leeds%201834%20to%202011%2011%20Dec%202011.pdf)
- Williams, J.E. (1971) 'The Leeds Corporation Strike in 1913' in Briggs, A. & Saville, J. (eds) *Essays in Labour History 1886-1923*, Archon Books: London
- Woodhouse, T. (1996) *Nourishing the Liberty Tree: Liberals and Labour in Leeds 1880-1914,* Keele University Press: Keele
- *Report of the Special Committee* (available in National Gas Archives)
- There is a small collection of items from the strike including a scrapbook of newspaper reports and photo of senior police officers held by the West Yorkshire Archive Service in Wakefield

Notes

1 This was not a straightforward process or one without numerous set backs. Two failed attempts took place at establishing independent working class political labour representation in Leeds before the Leeds ILP was established in 1893, and it took the ASE lockout of 1898 before many unions contemplated forming a Labour representation committee and there were still attempts to tie workers to winning over the Liberals and splits within socialist organisations.

2 This paper was actually based in Bradford rather than Leeds, but reported heavily on the dispute

3 Leeds Labour Party also published the Leeds Weekly Citizen

4 Militant was the forerunner organisation of the Socialist Party, to read more about the Liverpool Council struggle we recommend Peter Taaffe & Tony Mulhearn's *Liverpool: A City That Dared to Fight*

5 Ironically, it was the Michael Sadler building, named after this Vice Chancellor, that students at Leeds University chose to occupy in protest over plans to increase tuition fees in 2011

6 Was the decision of the tramwaymen to return to work to protect their jobs, and effectively abandon their fellow workers worth it? I have not yet been able to find records of what happened when their agreement with the council expired on 4th August 1914. However, this was same day the British ruling class faced more pressing concerns as the country declared war on Germany and joined the first world war, and therefore the result of any negotiations that could have taken place would have been heavily influenced by that factor. Arthur Gill, President of FCME was particularly bitter, raising the issue in his address to the 1914 AGM of Leeds Trades Council.

socialist books

All of the books listed below are available from Socialist Books.
To order further copies of this publication or any from either the list or the many other publications published by Socialist Books contact us at:

Socialist Books, PO Box 24697, London E11 1YD
telephone: 020 8988 8789 or **email:** socialistbooks@socialistparty.org.uk
or online at the socialist books **website:** www.socialistbooks.co.uk

recent titles available from socialist books

- **A Socialist World is Possible: The History of the CWI**
  by Peter Taaffe
  Published August 2004. 96 pages paperback
  An account and celebration of the activity and contribution of the Committee for a Workers International (CWI) on the 30 Anniversary of its founding, showing how the role and influence of the organisation has developed and change -, in some regions of the world quite dramatically - from its humble origins.
  Price £5.00

- **1926 General Strike Workers Taste Power**
  by Peter Taaffe
  Published May 2006. 192 pages paperback
  Written to commemorate the eightieth anniversary of the 1926 General Strike in Britain and, more importantly, to draw the lessons from this movement.
  Price £7.50

- **The Masses Arise The Great French Revolution 1789-1815**
  by Peter Taaffe
  Published June 2009. 166 pages paperback
  An understanding of the French Revolution remains crucial for all revolutionaries. Marx, Engels, Lenin and Trotsky studied it intensely to gain an understanding of the dynamics of revolutions.
  Price £10.00